LIVES ON THE MISSISSIPPI

LIVES ON THE MISSISSIPPI

Literature and Culture along the Great River from the Collections of the St. Louis Mercantile Library Association

A Checklist for an exhibition
held at the Grolier Club in New York
February 23 – May 1, 2010

St. Louis Mercantile Library
at the University of Missouri – St. Louis
2010

This exhibition was made possible in part through the generosity of the
Herman T. and Phenie R. Pott Foundation
and the Benton Roblee Duhme Fund

Foreword

Since 1846, the St. Louis Mercantile Library Association has witnessed the life and vitality of a young nation as it moved steadily forward, often on the waterways which delineated its historic city's boundaries. The leaders of the city who established this long lived frontier institution did so in part to commemorate the achievements of those they felt represented the past successes and triumphs of the nation – the stories of the entrepreneurs of the later west to be sure would be documented there, but the records were intended to include far more tales, those of the trappers and mountain men, the explorers and the railroad builders, and certainly the keel boat men, the river pilots and steamboat captains.

Today the Mercantile is a house with many rooms. Its great special collections focus on the American West, the history of railroading in America and the story of America's inland waterways, and are some of its strongest collections and those which have been built upon from the early days of the 1840s especially over the last twenty five years in order to create broad and deep, comprehensive collections for advanced scholars and general readers alike. The St. Louis Mercantile Library is proud to have been invited by the Grolier Club to showcase examples of one of its key special collections, that concerning the history of the Mississippi. Of course this is appropriate for an institution coming from the region of the Father of Waters, but the Mississippi is allegorical for much that was and is America as a whole and it is a pleasure to present something of this relationship to viewers.

I wish to thank the staff of the Grolier Club for its tremendous support of this exhibition, especially Eric Holzenberg and Megan Smith for their enthusiasm and advice. I would also like to thank Julie Dunn-Morton and Gregory Ames of the St. Louis Mercantile Library curatorial staff, as well as Page Choate and Loren McClain, Museum Studies graduate assistants at the Mercantile, and volunteers Ann and James Blum who have all worked very hard to make such an exhibition possible across many miles and through many long and exuberating hours of discovery. As usual, the Board of Direction of the St. Louis Mercantile Library Association, and its Pott Historic Waterways Collection advisory board have been supportive, generous and enthusiastic at all times regarding this project. To all my gratitude.

John Neal Hoover
Executive Director
St. Louis Mercantile Library Association

See Item 30

Introduction

Over the past thirty years at the St. Louis Mercantile Library I have been honored to have been associated with helping build what is now considered the largest American rail history collection in a North American Library. That collection was based mainly on the acquisition of the papers, books and historic photographs of one collector, John W. Barriger III, a depression era economic consultant turned rail executive, but the collection attracted even larger holdings of rail historical societies and libraries which were on the auction block, and corporate collections of photographs and plans needing a good home. Each new collection repeated certain similarities – the rail collections were mortared with carefully crafted business archives and bricked with corporate annual reports. No detail was too small and the glory of the Barriger collection is its comprehensiveness and depth from one railroad to the next, merger by merger, plan by plan.

As the rail collection grew in its early years at the Mercantile, the Library was under pressure to remember its mission to celebrate all the historic entrepreneurship of its region. Transportation history was coming full circle in our institution and I was assigned to create the beginnings of a comprehensive collection on the history of American inland waterways. I quickly learned that a collection on the history of American rivers, based in an ancient library on the banks of the Mississippi was as fluid an undertaking as such a subject might obviously suggest! Just as rigid and formal as the rail collections seemed in their rich arrays of timetables, charts and statistics, the collection and collectors which constitute a river historical collection are very different – older, scattered over the landscape of subjects, from natural history to technology over great stretches of time, jealously guarded by colorful gatekeepers who seek out every scrap of a mention of a steamboat wreck or a little known deckhand, pilot or passenger, in some respects livelier, full of contradictions, triumph and tragedy.

When one collects "the river", one finds oneself amidst many subjects at once – from early maps and flyaway accounts to snapshots, scrapbooks, folk art and the greatest examples of American literature. In examining "lives" on the Mississippi, one could launch into studying, say, the engineers and navigators, native Americans, immigrants to the promised lands of farms and industry along the river, African-American deckhands, itinerant artists and writers, folksingers and jazz musicians, soldiers, cartographers and explorers.

This exhibition attempts to outline a feel for that diversity of a two-thousand mile community through examining various recurrent formats which form the backbone of the Library's collection in maps, prints, paintings, books and artifacts to present a taste of a very broadly defined yet deep collection, still evolving as the river keeps "rolling along" through floods and better days, through history and memory. These formats include as well ledgers, papers, bills of lading, manifests and steamboat archives, blueprints and models, ephemera and travel brochures. The collection has been built upon the eyewitness collections of the Mercantile, founded at a time when steamboat whistles echoed in its streets, as well as latter day collectors – editors, teachers, journalists and amateur historians who have all shared their collections with the Mercantile.

See Item 8

Maps

The maps of the Mississippi River from the earliest times have a mystique, scale and interelationship unlike the rivers on any other continent and as cartographers grasped the significance of the incredible natural highways of North America, they conveyed this elegantly in these magisterial plates to their governments. The mapping of the river went on for centuries, always more detail, and with every flood and upheaval always more change.

(1) John Ross. *Course of the River Mississipi, from the Balise to Fort Chartres; Taken on an Expedition to the Illinois, in the latter end of the Year 1765.* (From: *The American Atlas* by Thomas Jefferys. London: Robert Sayer, 1775).

Based on surveys conducted only two years after the Treaty of Paris ceded lands east of the Mississippi to England, Lieutenant Ross's detailed map was a significant advance over the work of two distinguished French cartographers, D'Anville and Robert. Widely held to be the most reliable map of the river produced in the 18th century, it also evidences the Mississippi's growing social, political, commercial and agricultural significance.

(2) Myron Coloney & Sidney B. Fairchild. ***Ribbon Map of the Father of Waters.*** St. Louis: Gast, Moeller & Co., 1866.

Stretching to nearly 11 feet and mounted on linen, this patented "ribbon map" was marketed especially to tourists who – its inventors hoped – would enjoy seeing the passing panorama of towns, landings, plantations, and mileage points clearly and accurately identified. Though not a commercial success, ribbon maps were a remarkable representation of the rolling river that inspired them. Incredibly scarce today, this is one of a handful known and the only one possible to be effectively displayed. (Courtesy, Olin Library Special Collections, Washington University in St. Louis).

(3) Guillaume de l'Isle.***Carte de la Louisiane et du Cours du Mississipi. (From: Atlas Nouveau Contenant Toutes les Parties du Monde.*** Amsterdam: Covens and Mortier, 1742).

Guillaume de l'Isle's "Map of Louisiana and the Mississippi River" is one of the most famous maps in American history and what cartographers call a "mother map," one that spurs great imitation or innovation. Originally published in 1718, the year he was appointed "Chief Geographer to the King" (Louis XIV), this map was used for another half century and considered the most authoritative of the Mississippi Valley. It was also the first accurately to track the expeditions of Hernando De Soto, Henri de Tonty and Louis de St. Denis.

(4) John Senex. *A map of Louisiana and of the river Mississipi. 1719 (From: John Senex A New General Atlas,* London: Daniel Browne, Thomas Taylor, et al, 1721).

Senex borrowed liberally from Guillaume de l'Isle's *Carte de la Louisiane et du cours du Mississipi,* 1718, which also included the route of explorer Fernando de Soto. Senex's debt to de l'Isle did not, however, extend to reproducing French claims to Carolina. Ironically, this map is dedicated to William Law, the father of John Law, whose infamous "Mississippi Bubble" scheme proved the ruination of many Europeans of that period. (See Item 54)

(5) Zebulon Pike. Map of the Mississippi River from its Source to the Mouth of the Missouri. *(From: An account of expeditions to the sources of the Mississippi, and through the western parts of Louisiana, to the sources of the Arkansaw, Kans, La Platte, and Pierre Jaun, rivers.* Philadelphia: C. & A. Conrad & Co., 1810)

In 1805, as the Lewis & Clark expedition made its way westward, Lieutenant Zebulon Pike led a detachment of twenty soldiers northward from St. Louis to survey the upper Mississippi River and determine its source. Pike mistakenly identified Leech Lake in Minnesota as its source; it wasn't until 1832 that Lake Itasca, the true source of the river, was discovered by Henry Rowe Schoolcraft. Nevertheless, the map Pike produced was the most accurate to date as well as a model of the engraver's art.

(6) Herman Moll. *A New Map of the North Parts of America Claimed by France Under the Names of Louisiana, Mississipi, Canada and New France with the Adjoining Territories of England and Spain.* London: H. Moll and John King, 1720.

Moll, of Dutch or German origin, became one of England's most prominent cartographers, and his work was prized for its elegance. Here, as did his contemporary Senex (Item 4), Moll relies on de l'Isle's for his charting of the Mississippi River. Moll's friends included Daniel Defoe whose novel *Moll Flanders* may have derived its name from a well-known book of that time: *The History of Flanders with Moll's Map.* Moll was adamant about California being an island: "I have had in my office mariners who have sailed around it."

(7) John Baptist Homann. *Amplissima regionis Mississipi seu provinciae Ludovicianae â R. P. Ludovico Hennepin Francisc Miss. in America...*(From: *Atlas Geographicus Major Norimbergae Homannianis Heredibus.* Nuremberg: J. B. Homann, 1763).

A cartographic *tour de force,* based on Jesuit Father Louis Hennepin's narratives of La Salle's explorations, published in 1697, and de l'Isle's seminal map. Hennepin, depicted in the upper left corner, was among the first to describe Niagara Falls (also shown), as well as St. Anthony Falls, the only natural waterfall on the Mississippi. The source of the Mississippi is shown "based on the reports of Indians." Homann, a German cartographer, labels the land west of the Appalachians as *Louisiane,* thus prolonging the wrath of both England and Spain. Note that New Orleans is sited on the wrong side of the Mississippi.

(8) Georges H. V. Victor Collot. *A Journey in North America, Containing a Survey of the Countries Watered by the Mississippi, Ohio [etc.].* Paris: A. Bertrand, 1824-6. With copy of the centennial reprint published in Florence in 1924.

One of the three essential early descriptions of life in the early Mississippi Valley, a list including Henry Lewis' *Das Illustrirte Mississippithal* (See Item 68) and Lewis Thomas and John Caspar Wild's *Valley of the Mississippi Illustrated* (See Item 33). A work published a generation after General Collot surveyed the interior regions of Louisiana and the Mississippi, this book was planned for military intrigues and colonial contest, but transcended its purpose in documenting the earliest settlements of the French or "Illinois Country" of the late eighteenth century.

(9) Robert E. Lee. *Map of the Harbor of St. Louis. Washington,* D.C.: W. J. Stone, 1837.

Robert E. Lee arrived in St. Louis in 1837 as a thirty-year old 1st lieutenant with the Army Corps of Engineers and an engineering problem to solve. Growing sandbars and islands were limiting access to the city's levees; St. Louis's steamboat traffic and economy were imperiled. Lee and German-born engineer Henry Kayser devised a series of underwater jetties (depicted here) intended to divert stronger river currents toward the St. Louis side of the river. Although neither Congress nor the city of St. Louis could raise the funds to complete this project, Lee's work did, in Mayor John Darby's words, "preserve the harbor." Lee went on to improve the Mississippi's navigability at Keokuk, Iowa, an accomplishment that earned him the rank of captain.

(10) American Barge Line Co., Inc. ***Through Line Service.*** Ca. 1940.

This advertising map for the American Barge Line Co. reveals not only the economic importance of inland waterways, but the Mississippi River's ever-changing course, natural or man-made (see red-lettered note in mileage table). During the 1930s and 1940s, the U.S. Army Corps of Engineers created cutoffs which shortened the river by 150 miles, increased current speed and reduced flood levels. Formed in 1927, the American Barge Line Co. is now a subsidiary of American Commercial Lines, Inc., headquartered in Jeffersonville, Indiana. The company operates over 3,100 barges which haul grain, coal and other commodities totaling over 40 million tons of cargo per year.

(11) Jean-Hyacinthe Laclotte. ***Battle of New Orleans.*** (1815)

This panoramic view of the Battle of New Orleans (1815) serves as a reminder that the Mississippi River is also a major strategic artery, one desperately sought by the British in the last engagement of the War of 1812. Sketched at the battle and later painted by Laclotte (1765-1829), a French architect and assistant engineer serving in the Louisiana Army, this scene was widely available shortly after the battle through detailed prints. This descriptive key – in both English and French – likely accompanied them.

(12) Mississippi River Commission. ***Map of the Alluvial Valley of the Mississippi River From the Head of St. Francis Basin to the Gulf of Mexico Showing Lands Subject to Overflow, Location of Levees and Trans-Alluvial Overflow.*** St. Louis: Stephens Lithography and Engraving Co., 1887.

The awareness that planning could somehow relieve flooding lulled residents of the Mississippi River into a feeling of false security, leading to disastrous results every few years down to the present day. Maps of this sort were reminders and warnings that only constant vigilance and upkeep would delay the day the folksongs always foretold "when the levee breaks". This map was indeed forgotten, rolled, folded over on its roll, boxed for generations and stored in a loft of the Mercantile, only to be rediscovered and restored a century after it was printed in St. Louis.

Prints, Drawings, Paintings, Broadsides, Posters

See Item 25

Prints, Drawings, Paintings, Broadsides, Posters

The visual record of the Mississippi has been a special collecting interest of the Mercantile Library. From the days when it was Bingham's first patron, the institution collected icons of the river such as the artist's sketchbook of people on the waterways and in the river towns and his Jolly Flat Boat Men in Port. That tradition continues with the acquisition of modern art and photographs which document this compelling river world.

(13) Karl Bodmer. ***Tower Rock, View on the Mississippi.*** Coblenz: Hoelscher, 1839-41.

The ninth vignette included in the Atlas to Prince Maximilian of Wied-Neuwied's *Travels in the Interior of North America, 1832-1834.* As key a document as this work has become related to the study of Native Americans, it is often overlooked as equally useful for a depiction of virtually all early American waterways. It married effectively and eloquently the lives of Indians as bound up with the Father of Waters.

(14) After George Caleb Bingham. ***Bound Down the River.*** New York: Nathaniel T. Currier and James M. Ives, 1870.

By the time this print was designed, the era of the keel boats and their boisterous and intrepid crews was a fading memory. Even Bingham's masterpiece oils of the 1850s on the same subject, the most important of which was preserved at the St. Louis Mercantile Library for generations before being transferred to the St. Louis Art Museum to be shown to a wider audience, were narratives of a bygone life and pioneering spirit that a new generation felt should be, thankfully, preserved for a national, ongoing consciousness.

(15) Currier & Ives. ***Great Fire at St. Louis, 1849.*** New York: 1849.

Part of the rite of passage of a great American city in the 19th century seemed to be a conflagration of this dramatic sort. During a particularly frightening May of cholera and financial panic and risk, the steamboat-hemmed riverfront of warehouses and businesses caught fire from boat to boat and building to building, eventually enveloping the entire central city–the printing establishment of the early community was reported swept away; however, Mercantile Library files reveal extras were out on the street within seventy two hours.

(16) Edouard Lamasson (possibly Henry Lewis). ***St. Louis Riverfront after the Great Fire of 1849,*** ca. 1849.

This mysterious watercolor may have been part of a river panorama or a sketch of a proposed one. It is unsigned and attached documentation with the "Lamasson" attribution only makes the work more confusing. The panorama artist and painter, Lewis, left identical sketch books and his family retained evidence that the artist may have toyed with signing his name as "Lamasson" or "Lemasson". What is significant is that this is as close as most 21st century people will ever get to the newsreel immediacy of those 19th century "paintings by the mile", the great Mississippi River panoramas which toured the world until nearly all of them were worn out, cut down into panels or screens or wallpaper, or thrown away. This fragment of American river history has been pre-served over the Mercantile Library's front door through three buildings and eight generations.

(17) George Catlin. ***St. Louis in 1832.*** 1832. St. Louis: St. Louis Mercantile Library Association, 1856 (William K. Bixby Bequest)

The Mercantile Library in St. Louis was host to many art fairs and wel-comed itinerant artists on their way west in the days of the frontier. Many of these painters took time out to paint the Mississippi and the great port and gateway to uncharted territory. Catlin created two paint-ings of this cheery scene from an unusual perspective – no artist ever attempted a south view again – and in the process provided the earliest urban view of the city, which this subsequent print (from one of the two sketches at that time in the Mercantile's possession) documented.

(18) Hatch & Co. New York. *The Robert E. Lee.* New Orleans: Stetson & Armstrong, 1865

Lithographed by the firm of Hatch and Company in New York, this is one of the rarest of steamboat advertising prints and one commemorating the yet to be won great steamboat race between this great vessel and the *Natchez* from New Orleans to St. Louis in 1870, when the unthinkable speed on the Mississippi of thirteen miles per hour was attained as the new record. All the captains raced, sometimes with disastrous results. The race between the *Natchez* and the *Lee* passed into lore and legend which in part obscured the reality of the dangers of river travel at its apex.

(19) *Steamer Grand Republic.* Boston: Forbes Company, Ca. 1880.

The sheer size of the steamboat "floating palaces" cannot be overestimated, even by modern standards. On the early Mississippi they must have stood out as behemoths of progress and grace for all. The *Grand Republic* was one of the largest of these and such posters advertised its speed, capacity, efficiency and comfort.

(20) Camille N. Dry and Richard J. Compton. *Pictorial St. Louis: The Great Metropolis of the Mississippi Valley: A Topographical Survey Drawn in Perspective AD 1875.* St. Louis: Compton and Company, 1876.

This remarkable book is an indigenous treasure of Mississippi Valley printing. A comprehensive series of birds-eye elevations taken from hot air balloons were transferred to stone to produce one of the first detailed comprehensive views of the river metropolis. Equivalent to the widespread county atlases of the era, each house, each street, each steamboat is identified by name and property owner and everyone bought a copy. Most books did not survive due to the cumbersome size and poor quality of paper and binding, but when one turns up it is always an event; the Mercantile possesses multiple sets in various bindings and colored and uncolored formats.

(21) *The Bombardment and Capture of Fort Hindman, Arkansas Post, Ark. Jany. 11th 1863.* New York: Currier and Ives, 1863.

The systematic sweeping of the Mississippi of Confederate control during the Civil War took place in well orchestrated naval operations such as this. The Mississippi was an inceptive setting of modern naval warfare, so often dependent on newly mechanized innovation of power and destruction. How the dwellers must have longed for the reassuring and cheerful whistles of the packet boats, the peaceful travel denied a blockaded Mississippi during the war.

(22) *Siege of Vicksburg.* Chicago: Kurz and Allison, 1888.

One of the score-plus Civil War chromolithographs of the noted Chicago print makers, this commemorative depiction of the joint naval and army operation led by Grant at the Confederate stronghold. The turning point of the Civil War hinged on the free and open navigation of the Mississippi under Union control. (Gift of James Shiele)

(23) Thomas Hart Benton. *The Flood.* 1937.

Benton's regionalist angst and outrage never shone through better than when he could crusade on the plight of the people along the Mississippi affected by the devastating floods of the 1920s and during the Depression, as evidenced in this important print.

(24) John Stuart Curry. *Sanctuary.* 1944.

Lives along the Mississippi included all lives and the artists knew this. In the early part of the 20th century printmakers, scientists, engineers, children's authors – all of them – horrified by the ecological disaster caused by denuding the Mississippi River Valley of its flora and fauna, and witness to the rage of reactive floods of Mother Nature, went on a campaign for better management of the resources of the great river valley. Here is the famous Associated American Artist's print by Curry, perhaps the most eloquent voice of all.

(25) Joe Jones. *St. Louis Riverfront.* 1932.

This charcoal sketch was made for a subsequent oil. Collected during the 1930s at an art sale by the original owner (she had to hide it in her room from her parents, horrified that they might find out she spent 40 dollars) directly from the famous crusading artist and activist, the work achieves the simulation of motion and activity in just a few lines of what generations of artists attempted unsuccessfully in scores of other Mississippi river city views.

(26) Thomas Hart Benton. ***Down the River.*** 1939.

Benton returned over and over again in his work to fishing scenes of the Mississippi backwaters and those of the Ozarks. Often these compositions were reworked for his seminal illustrations of classic volumes, such as *Life on the Mississippi* and *Huckleberry Finn.*

(27) Thomas Hart Benton. ***Towboat.*** 1935-1940.

This original pencil and ink sketch by Benton marks the passing of steam to diesel power just as surely as earlier artists noted in their work the demise of the keelboat age on the Mississippi.

(28) Otto Kuhler. ***On the Levee – Memphis, Tenn.*** 1929.

Kuhler, in his etchings of the American landscape, was always interested in industry and productivity and poetically here conveys that powerful message by depicting the sheer size of an inland waterfront cargo on the way to deep water ports.

(29) Frederick Oakes Sylvester. ***The Great River.*** Chicago: Frederick Oakes Sylvester, 1911.

Sylvester was a leading figure in the arts of his adopted region of the central Mississippi Valley. He founded the Art School of Principia College in Illinois and for years created tremendously romantic impressions in oil and verse of the Mississippi which culminated in this humble book of poems which is a Holy Grail to the regional river collectors. For the limited version of the first edition the artist supplied watercolor frontispieces of river landscapes near his artist's retreat above Alton, Illinois. In large towns like St. Louis, Sylvester created vivid murals of the bucolic river bluffs of the region as well as atmospheric scenes of steamers, bridges, water and mist. (See Item 35)

(30) Thomas Doney, after George Caleb Bingham. ***The Jolly Flat Boat Men.*** New York: American Art Union, 1847.

The Doney mezzotint and engraving preserved this most famous of Bingham images after the original painting fell for a time into obscurity as is so often the case with 19th century American genre painting. Another version of the painting, however, hung for generations in the reading room of the St. Louis Mercantile Library Association. Such river paintings made the reputation of Bingham in his day and make his art supremely worthwhile in the present to a world viewership which is drawn into the life of the Mississippi through this archetypical design.

(31) John James Audubon. ***The Birds of America; from Original Drawings.*** London: Published by the Author, 1827-1838. With Audubon's ***Ornithological Biography.*** Edinburgh: Black, 1835, volumes I and III (of five).

"The Great Blue Heron", Plate CCXI *"Their contours and movements are always graceful, if not elegant...How calm, how silent, how grand is the scene! The tread of the tall bird himself no one hears, so carefully does he place his foot on the moist ground, cautiously suspending it for a while at each step of his progress." – John James Audubon*

This is one of only three reserved copies of the original double elephant folio edition of Audubon's masterpiece. It passed down from in-laws of the Berthoud family in the Mississippi valley to the Mercantile Library in St. Louis in 1858 and it is an inscribed and signed set. It is a reminder for this exhibition of the warm welcome and aid the naturalist received from friends along the Mississippi as Audubon went about collecting specimens and sketches of the profuse species he encountered from the wilderness head waters to the delta, from the mouths of the great tributaries like the Ohio, Illinois and Missouri rivers to the back inlets, bays and marshes, some of the richest living ecosystems on the face of the planet.

(32) Claude Regnier, after George Caleb Bingham. ***In a Quandary. Mississippi Raftsmen Playing Cards***. New York and Paris: Goupil and Co. 1852.

In the 1940's and 1950's, one of the largest industrial companies along the Mississippi initiated a program to reprint and preserve the key river scenes of the 19th century, which were even then disappearing into corporate collections and museums certainly at best, but more likely becoming forgotten and discarded from the walls and attics of the houses of past settlers by their descendants. This version of the Regnier print of a genre scene of raftsmen's "affairs", showing the rustic genre of the region as it moved into history is one of these, published by the Mississippi Lime Company of Alton, Illinois, and collectors in the region are more excited by that imprint than the original due to local spirit which sometimes slips into the collecting impulse. This company reproduced excellent versions of nearly one hundred river related scenes.

(33) John Caspar Wild. ***View of Carondelet; South St. Louis.*** 1841.

This watercolor view of the riverfront just south of St. Louis in Carondelet village is one of the artist's only surviving works and designs for the many lithographs he published at the same time in a key Midwestern rarity, The *Valley of the Mississippi Illustrated* (See Item 8). About this scene from that text: "Its site occupies a slope...that rises like an amphitheatre from the water...the village is regularly laid out, in blocks of about three hundred feet, in each of which there is generally a house of logs or weather boarding, surrounded with an orchard and garden; the whole presenting a very rural and picturesque appearance. Still so today, this scene and bend in the Mississippi rises up immediately to greet the motorist heading south on Broadway in an impressive and nostalgically dramatic fashion linking the present with the past.

(34) *Fitch's Last Model of a Steam Engine in the Possession of the St. Louis Mercantile Library.* ca. 1865

A broadside printed in the mid nineteenth century by the St. Louis Mercantile Library has hung at the Library for generations, long after the model disappeared, and is evocative of the spirited ways in which the old mercantile libraries and their leaders used such settings to study and analyze progress as applied in their day, by commemorating the work of past inventors and entrepreneurs whose innovations, such as John Fitch's steamboats meant to the heartland's river system.

(35) Frederick Oakes Sylvester. *St. Louis Riverfront.* 1901.

Sylvester was one of the greatest painters of the Mississippi, studying art first in Massachusetts and next teaching at Newcomb in New Orleans. By the time he came to Principia in Illinois he grasped his life work of celebrating the many moods, colors and impressions of the river. Here in this view of the industrial port of St. Louis–a riverfront abandoned as a subject since Bingham's time, becoming more a back door to others, the visionary artist created an idyll of the river in harmony with the city in a positive canvass of late afternoon light and golden haze, which belied the gritty realities of coal smoke, noise and hustle in favor of a placid, peaceful riverfront.

(36) John Caspar Wild. *View of St. Louis from the South of Chouteau's Lake.* St. Louis: Missouri Republican Office, 1840.

This is one of the rarest lithographic views of the early river town, taken in perspective by the town booster, Wild, from a backwater slough long drained for a railroad terminal, but is included for the charming scene of what recreational life along the Mississippi must have been like at one time.

Photographs

See Item 40

Photographs

The great collectors of Mississippi river history always have three things: a card file of steamboats and participants, books and papers concerning favorite boats, and piles of photographs of early boats and captains on the river. The Mercantile has continued to expand the collections as they become available.

(37) *First Iron-Clad Built in America: U.S. Gunboat "St. Louis" Now Called "De Kalb".* St. Louis: James B. Eads, 1863.

This commemorative photograph of James Eads' first Iron Clad shows a moment when launched as one of the key turning points of the Civil War, when Unionists used technology and the mind of the great engineer to break the deadlock on the Mississippi by the Confederacy.

(38) Emil Boehl. **Robert E. Lee.** 1870.

Boehl grew up in St. Louis at the time of the great early photographers, learning from Thomas Easterly and the rest and thus had a penchant for documentary photography, eventually leaving us thousands of images.

(39) Ruth Ferris. **Deckhands.** Ca. 1935.

This photograph was taken at the end of the steam packet era by an elementary school teacher who amassed one of the great collections of Mississippi River lore.

(40) Ruth Ferris. **Marking Twain** (2 photographs). Ca. 1940.

Perhaps the most significant photographs taken by Ferris were her series of deckhand studies including a series of river men throwing lead lines to "mark twain" and take river depths. These images may be unique to the practice which provided one of the greatest of all pen names. (See Item 123)

(41) *Boehl and Koenig. Steamboats – War Eagle, Mattie Bell, Dacotah, and the Belle of Shreveport.* Ca. 1879.

Some of the grand "floating palaces" captured in less auspicious times and surroundings awaiting repairs and traveling orders.

(42) *Lake Superior: St. Louis and St. Paul Northern Line Passenger Packet.* Ca. 1870

The *Lake Superior* packet once carried 800 tons of silver ore from St. Paul to St. Louis. In 1879 the ship burned with the *Dubuque* in Alton while being readied for the a new transport season. The blaze was said to have begun in *Lake Superior's* barbershop.

(43) *Mississippi River Commission Photographs,* Ca. 1898-99

This extraordinary 19th century photo album of working prints that was used to study the lower Mississippi and delta areas is opened to two main concerns of the old river commission – the protection of nature and the effective face of industry. These glimpses of activity and commerce were captured by an anonymous engineer. (Presented to the Mercantile Library by Washington University)

(44) Marga Sachse Finger *Snapshots Scrapbook.* 1947.

This humble snapshot album brought to a close over a century of regular river passenger service on the Mississippi and documents the end of an era and a fascinating way of life. As Mrs. Finger, a passenger and witness wrote in the album: *On May 18, 1947, at 2:30 a.m., the "Golden Eagle" tore a hole in her hull at Grand Tower Island* (See Item 13)*, in the Mississippi River. A heavy jolt awakened nearly everyone aboard after the first hours of sound sleep. A jolly crowd of 45 guests, including many seasoned steamboat fans, had just started on a seven day trip to Nashville, Tenn. It had been a day of travel, a gala dinner on board, and an evening of fun and entertainment for all. About 15 minutes after the crash all passengers were asked to dress and get ready to leave the boat."* The pilothouse of the steamer was eventually saved and preserved in St. Louis on a children's playground, until being transferred to the Missouri Historical Society. The plans, extensive photos and records of the vessel are preserved at the Mercantile Library.

(45) John A. Fox. *Mississippi River Flood Problem: How the Floods can be Prevented.* Washington, D.C.: J.W. Bryan Press, 1914.

With a photographic frontispiece depicting flood victims as refugees of the wild river torrents which regularly subjected communities to devastation, this is one of scores of case statements and position papers leading to more effective federal intervention in flood control and levee construction.

(46) J.H. Fitzgibbon. *Eads Bridge Under Construction.* Ca. 1873.

A remarkable photograph of the Eads Bridge nearing completion, it depicts one of the great American spans of any kind and the first important steel construction. The bridge was the first to provide both rail and vehicular traffic and was many times larger than any bridge up to its time. Still in perfect use after nearly 140 years, the Eads Bridge is a monument to its engineer and a marvel of elegant design simplicity produced on a massive scale.

See Item 54

Books

The books in these cases are representative of a deep collection developed over time across many subjects that connect the themes of life, history and culture to the Mississippi. A collection to be read and referenced by a broad public in the 19th century – the affairs of the Mississippi were often the affairs of the day in general – the collections in later times grew and expanded into a scholarly research collection which is one of the largest of its kind.

AWARENESS AND EXPLORATION

The early books collected on the Mississippi are romantic ones of personal adventure, exploration and discovery, and mark a time and an age when the continent was new, and its river system one of myth and legend carried to the coasts by natives' word of mouth. European books documented a world that was very unfamiliar, but full of promise and wealth.

(47) M. Bossu. *Nieuwe reizen naer Noord-Amerika: behelzende eene beschryving van de onderscheidene volken en stammen, die de landen omtrend de grote rivier Saint Louis, gewoonlyk de Mississipi genaamd, bewoonen, derzelver Godsdienst, staatsbestuur, zeden, wyze van oorlogen en koophandel: in 't Fransch beschreeven / door den heere Bossu; en nu volgens den Parysschen druk in 't Nederduitsch vertaald; met plaaten.* Amsterdam: Steven van Esveldt, 1769.

The Dutch edition of an international bestseller in the eighteenth century on life in the Mississippi Valley at mid-century by a soldier who was stationed among the Indian tribes from Fort Chartres in Illinois to New Orleans.

(48) Louis Hennepin. *Beschryving van Louisania : nieuwelijks ontdekt ten zuidwesten van Niew-Vrankryk, door order van den Koning / met de kaart des landts, en een nauwkeurige verhandeling van de zeden en manieren van leeven der wilden.* T'Amsterdam: Jan ten Hoorn, 1688.

First Dutch edition of the most important writings of a missionary who saw much and reported even more, often not to his credit. (See Item 52) International editions such as this show the extreme interest in describing and marketing the New World – the world of the Mississippi was alive with travelers, soldiers and claimants to its potential wealth.

(49) Daniel Defoe. ***The Chimera, or, The French Way of Paying National Debts, Laid Open: Being an Impartial Account of the Proceedings in France, for Raising a Paper Credit, and Settling the Mississippi Stock.*** London: T. Warner, 1720.

Defoe, always in his day a keen observer of finance, was aghast in this pamphlet concerning John Law's "consultancy" with the French government, which was calculated to aid that nation's balance of credit, severely weakened as it was by years of Louis XIV's wars. Law based his economics on paper credit, as related to, most fatefully, the Mississippi Company. Nothing was backed by precious metals however; land rushes in the New World at first helped France but eventually a monumental collapse occurred, ruining all associated with the scheme.

(50) Jacques Marquette. ***Ontdekking va eenige landen en volkeren, in 't noorder-gedeelte van America/ door P. Marquette en Joliet; geddan in het jaar 1673.*** Te Leyden: Pieter Vander Aa, 1707.

The Vander Aa edition of Marquette and Joliet's travels in the Mississippi Valley with the early maps of the region, some of the first.

(51) Antoine François de Laval. ***Voyage de la Louisiane, fait par ordre du roy en l'année mil sept cent vingt: dans lequel sont traitées diverses matières de physique, astronomie, géographie et marine : l'on y a joint les Observations sur la refraction, faites a Marseille, avec des reflexions sur ces observations ; divers voyages faits pour la correction de la carte de la côte de Provence ; des Reflexions sufr quelques points du sisteme de m. Newton / par le P. Laval.*** Paris: J. Mariette, 1728.

By the scientist of the expedition to first describe for the French government in detail the mouth of the Mississippi and the coast of Louisiana.

(52) Louis Hennepin. ***Description de la Louisiane, nouvellement decouverte au sud' oüest de la Nouvelle France / par ordre du roy. Avec la carte du pays: Les moeurs & la maniere de vivre des sauvages. Dediée a Sa Majesté par le R.P. Loüis Hennepin, missionaire Recollet & notaire apostolique.*** Paris: A. Auroy, 1688.

Hennepin's books were important for many firsts: use of the word "Louisiana" for one. His maps are important works. Accompanying La Salle to the Illinois River in 1679, at that point Hennepin split off from the main expedition and ascended the Mississippi witnessing for the first time by a white man a river that the Indians reverenced as much as any seventeenth century priest did the beliefs of Christianity.

(53) Philip Pittman. *The present state of the European settlements on the Mississippi: with a geographical description of that river illustrated by plans and draughts.* London: Printed for J. Nourse, 1770.

This is the most important description of English settlements in the trans-Appalachian region and the Mississippi Valley in the eighteenth century with thoroughly delineated river maps of great strategic need and use.

(54) John Law. *Groote Tafereel, Het, der Dwaasheid, vertoonende de opkomst, voortgang en ondergang der Actie Bubbel en Windnegotie, in Vrankryk, Engeland, en de Nederlanden, gepleegt in den Jaare MDCCXX.* 1720.

An acerbic collection of tracts, caricatures and satires laying waste to the failed French Mississippi Company – the "Mississippi Bubble" schemes – of the early 1700s, at least it made the name of the great river an international household word at such an pearly date. Displayed is an unrecorded image of the financial expert, Scotsman John Law, as the "king of kings" of the Mississippi, this volume is of immense interest in studying the early perceptions and popular European culture surrounding a remote wilderness of the time. (See Item 49)

(55) Thomas Jefferys. *The Natural and Civil History of the French Dominions in North and South America.* London: T. Jefferys, 1760.

Planned to document the tumultuous fall of French Quebec, but also with a copious section on Louisiana, this is a monumental work for its time on life in the Mississippi Valley. Jefferys also produced one of the most important American atlases of his day. (See Item 1)

See Item 60

Search for the Source

The search for a little pond in the north country which could be seen as the beginning of the great river was a Holy Grail for decades and a quest not only to find the Mississippi's source, but to link thus all its great tributaries and by extension all the waterways of America.

(56) Captain Willard Glazier. ***Headwaters of the Mississippi.*** Chicago: Rand McNally, 1894.

No modesty here...Captain Glazier insisted that the source of the Mississippi was correctly...Lake Glazier, and he spent a great deal of time writing books to prove the point based on presupposed mistakes of earlier explorers.

(57) Captain Willard Glazier. ***Down the Great River.*** Philadelphia: Hubbard Brothers, 1893.

Glazier's historical and anecdotal camping trip from the "true" source to New Orleans. One of the first "on the road" books describing the river as it changes at every bend.

(58) Henry R. Schoolcraft. ***Narrative Journal of Travels Through the Northwestern Regions of the United States From Detroit Through the Great Chain of American Lakes to the Sources of the Mississippi River.*** Albany: Hosford, 1821.

The first account of Schoolcraft's travels to Lake Itasca and the sources of the Mississippi. Copy of John Mason Peck, who, along with Timothy Flint, Lyman Draper, and Schoolcraft formed a group of early writers and scholars who continually celebrated the riparian regions in which they lived and worked.

(59) Giacomo Constantino Beltrami. ***La Découverte des Sources du Mississippi et de la Rivière Sanglante.*** Nouvelle Orléans: B. Levy, 1824.

Beltrami was an interesting figure on the early frontier. He intrepidly came to America to write a book of travels and made his way to the headwaters of the Mississippi, where he attached himself to government expeditions in progress. He was caught up in the interest in reaching the source of the Mississippi in his spirited books.

(60) Giacomo Constantino Beltrami. ***A Pilgrimage in Europe and America: Leading to the Discovery of the Sources of the Mississippi and Bloody River; with a Description of the Whole Course of the Former and of the Ohio.*** London: Hunt and Clarke, 1828.

Beltrami's enlarged edition of his travels, this time including detailed maps and plates.

THE
NAVIGATOR:

CONTAINING DIRECTIONS FOR NAVIGATING

THE

MONONGAHELA, OHIO, AND
ALLEGHANY, MISSISSIPPI

RIVERS;

WITH AN AMPLE ACCOUNT

OF THESE MUCH ADMIRED WATERS,

FROM THE

HEAD OF THE FORMER TO THE MOUTH OF THE LATTER;

AND A CONCISE DESCRIPTION

OF THEIR

TOWNS, VILLAGES, HARBOURS, SETTLEMENTS, &c.

———

WITH ACCURATE MAPS OF THE OHIO AND MISSISSIPPI.

———

TO WHICH IS ADDED

An Appendix,

CONTAINING

AN ACCOUNT OF LOUISIANA,

AND OF

THE MISSOURI AND COLUMBIA RIVERS,

AS DISCOVERED BY THE VOYAGE UNDER

CAPTAINS LEWIS AND CLARK.

———

SIXTH EDITION—IMPROVED AND ENLARGED,

———

PITTSBURGH,

PUBLISHED BY ZADOK CRAMER AND SOLD AT HIS
BOOKSTORE, MARKET-STREET.
[PRICE ONE DOLLAR.]

———

FROM THE PRESS OF CRAMER & SPEAR......1808.

See Item 63

Immigration

Books on the Mississippi and its river towns in the 19th century were great promoters of settlement. It was the great valley of the world, and boasted as the true land of plenty. This was the impetus behind much of the art, the panoramas, and the illustrated books and travel accounts of the period.

(61) John Banvard. ***Description of Banvard's Geographical Panorama of the Mississippi River.*** Boston: John Putnam, Printer, 1847.

The program for viewing Banvard's three mile panorama depicting a thousand mile of river life in his day. Such productions were the first "motion pictures" as scenes were slowly unwound in special theatres. Note that Mike Fink, the legendary and bigger than life boatman was featured as a special guest appearance in the narrative.

(62) Daniel Drake. ***Remarks on the Importance of Promoting Literary and Social Concert in the Valley of the Mississippi: as a Means of Elevating its Character, and Perpetuating the Union.*** Louisville, KY: Literary Convention of Kentucky, at the office of the Louisville Herald, 1833.

Already by the 1830s enough solidarity of spirit and cohesiveness in trade and culture led Drake, an Ohio physician, to believe that if a dissolution of the Union would occur, the settlers of the trans-Appalachians and the populace of the Mississippi Valley could weather such a storm in a new confederacy of common aid and interest. The work was suppressed due to its anticipation of the impending disaster of the Civil War and breakup of the Union, and is of great rarity. It points to the independence and economic progress of the region for settlement.

(63) Zadok Cramer. ***The Navigator.*** Pittsburgh: Zadok Cramer, 1808.

Cramer provided the first accurate, detailed navigational guides for the Ohio and Mississippi and to hold a copy of *The Navigator* is to commune with the early rush of humanity coursing from Marietta to Kentucky and Missouri in the first great rush of settlement after the Revolution in the Old Northwest. This is the fourth edition, not the sixth as proclaimed, and it is the first of these humble and well used books to make mention of the travels of Lewis and Clark up the great tributary on the other side of the Mississippi. Other early *Navigators* are here displayed. Several other series of river guides appeared after these up to the mid-nineteenth century, but Cramer's work will always be viewed as seminal to the growth and initial understanding of the early waterways as the roadway through the young nation.

(64) Andrew Ellicott. ***The Journal of Andrew Ellicott.*** Philadelphia: Budd & Bartram, 1803.

Sabin wrote of this work that it was "one of the earliest books by an American author which describes the vast regions [of the lower Mississippi and the Gulf] then desert and now teeming with life, activity and civilization." Ellicott was appointed Commissioner to determine the boundary between Spanish Florida and the U.S. and at the time it was published by this pioneer of the Mississippi Valley, as he was called, it was a major American sourcebook concerning Louisiana at the time of Jefferson's Purchase.

(65) Richard Risley and John Rowson Smith. ***Professor Risley and Mr. J.R. Smith's Original Gigantic Moving Panorama of the Mississippi River: Extending from the Falls of St. Anthony to the Gulf of Mexico.*** London: J.K. Chapman and Co., 1849.

Smith's panorama program claimed a depiction of four thousand miles, obviously including every bend and slough to be able to make that claim. One wishes for a chance to have seen such a massive work. The several panorama programs which have been preserved seem to indicate that they are almost as scarce as the lost original panoramas themselves.

(66) *Pomarede's Original Panorama of the Mississippi River.* 1849.

Of great interest in Pomarede's program of his river panorama are the wood engraved illustrations, helping approximate the designs of the painting just as in Lewis' *Illustrirte Mississippithal,* but on a more modest scale. Much Indian lore here – Leon Pomarede was one of the earliest painters in St. Louis who travelled west to paint, came back, settled down to decorating St. Louis Cathedral and other key structures like Henry Shaw's Linnean House on the grounds of the Missouri Botanical Garden, falling off a scaffold eventually to end his talented career.

(67) John Caspar Wild. *The valley of the Mississippi: illustrated in a series of views embracing pictures of the principal cities and towns, public buildings, and remarkable and picturesque scenery on the Ohio and Mississippi Rivers.* St. Louis, MO: J.C. Wild, 1841.

Wild's plates of the river and the communities he visited adorn the promotional themes of this extreme rarity. This work, along with Victor Collot and Henry Lewis stand as the three crucial documentary printed sources of the Mississippi. (See Item 33)

(68) Henry Lewis. *Das illustrirte Mississippithal: dargestellt in 80 nach der natur aufgenommenen ansichten vom wasserfalle zu St. Anthony an bis zum gulf von Mexico.* Düsseldorf: Arnz & Comp., 1857.

The Mercantile Library's two copies of this great Midwestern rarity. Lewis (See Item 16) was a house painter in early St. Louis turned panorama artist and his great work as unfurled on huge spindles played to royalty and average folk alike and encouraged especially German immigration and settlement along the Mississippi. Issued in twenty parts, the handful of surviving copies vary in terms of order, but the work approximates clearly what Lewis's huge panorama depicted from Minnesota to New Orleans. The half title and the image of the Piasa Bird are presented Up to historic times a huge glyptic image could be seen incised into the towering limestone river bluffs just above Alton of a mythical dragon/bird which preyed on the original inhabitants until destroyed by heroes. Lewis attempted to show events, history, folklore and commercial progress in the eighty plates which comprise this volume.

A shelf of books across the centuries bringing people face to face with the world of the Mississippi River:

(69a) Samuel R. Brown. *The Western Gazetteer; or Emigrant's Directory.* Auburn, NY: H.C. Southwick, 1817

(69b) Henry Marie Brackenridge. *Views of Louisiana, Together with a Journal of a Voyage up the Missouri River, in 1811.* Pittsburgh: Cramer, 1814

(69c) Timothy Flint. *The History and Geography of the Mississippi Valley. To Which is Appended a Condensed Physical Geography of the Atlantic United States, and the Whole American Continent.* Cincinnati: E.H. Flint; Boston: Carter, Hendee, and Co., 1833.

(69d) Louis Hennepin. *Nouveau voyage d'un pais plus grand que l'Europe: avec les reflections des enterprises du Sieur de la Salle, sur les mines de St. Barbe, &c.* Utrecht: A. Schouten, 1698.

(69e) *Ausführliche historische und geographische beschreibung des an dem grossen flusse Mississipi in Nord-America gelegenen hherrlichen landes Louisiana.* Leipzig: J.F. Gleditschens seel. sohn, 1720.

See Item 74

Steam

The life and activity of the river depended on steam and steamboats whistling around every bend, hemming every city three deep in harbors and this case presents some of the books documenting this world. Other sources, for example, were the newspapers of the great days of the river packets. News correspondents were assigned in every major city to write copiously of the comings and goings of the steamboats and their colorful and captivating crews, led by captains and pilots who could make as much as 1000 dollars in wages in a year in the 1840s, an unbelievably high paying job.

(70) Jean-Baptiste Marestier. ***Memoire sur les bateaux vapeur des Etats-Unis d'Amerique.*** Paris: de l'Imprimerie Royale, 1824.

A contemporary and definitive account of the first steamboats, the most important work of its day and of enormous influence on the world of steam transportation.

(71) John Fitch. ***The Original Steam-boat Supported; or, A Reply to Mr. James Rumsey's Pamphlet.*** Philadelpia: Z. Poulson, Jr. 1788.

The true inventor of the practical and successful conveyances known as steamboats. Fitch's work manifested itself in short order and the first steamboat appeared on the Mississippi as early as 1811.

(72) James T. Lloyd. ***Lloyd's Steamboat Directory, and Disasters on the Western Waters.*** Cincinnati: J.T. Lloyd & Co., 1856.

Steamboat disasters were a measured hazard always of this mode of travel, especially with captains dangerously competing to see who was speediest on the river, literally and daily gambling with passengers lives "to take the horns", to win the right to advertise as the swiftest boat on the western waters.

(73) Emerson W. Gould. ***Fifty Years on the Mississippi; or, Gould's History of River Navigation.*** Saint Louis, Nixon-Jones Printing Co., 1889.

One of the most important contemporary accounts of boats and river people, this book became a bible to collectors and historians of the river as a model for twentieth century collecting and preserving river history.

(74) Taylor and Crook. ***Sketch Book of Saint Louis.*** Saint Louis: George Knapp & Co., Printers and Binders, 1858.

Shown are plates of working vessels designed by Eads, in some of the engineer's earliest ventures – snag sweepers and wreck salvagers.

See Item 80

Bridges and Navigation

The history of the Mississippi in urban centers like Memphis, New Orleans and St. Louis was measured by shrill cries and jeremiads to quick and unimpeded navigation. What was good for the steamboat companies – like General Motors in later times – was good for the nation. In the center of all of this activity stood a gifted engineer of much conviction and pride, James Eads, and his great bridge.

(75) Joseph J. Brown and Sylvester Waterhouse. ***Give Us an Unobstructed Mississippi: A Memorial to Congress to Secure an Adequate Appropriation for a Prompt and Thorough Improvement of the Mississippi River.*** St. Louis: John J. Daly & Co., Printers, 1877.

An oft heard outcry. Waterhouse was an early academic from Washington University.

(76) Thomas M. Gunter. ***Speech of Hon. Thomas M. Gunter, of Arkansas, in the House of Representatives.*** Washington, D.C.: 1882.

On the flyleaf: "The Mississippi must be made navigable at all times, its overflow restrained, and its valley reclaimed, let the cost be what it may!"

(77) ***Delays at Upper Mississippi Bridges.*** Letter from the Secretary of War, 1876.

An act in Congress for securing boom arms to bridge piers for relieving log traffic in congested areas.

(78) Mississippi River Flood Control Association. ***Losses and Damages Resulting from the Flood of 1927, Mississippi River and Tributaries, in the States of Illinois, Missouri, Kentucky, Tennessee, Arkansas, Mississippi and Louisiana.*** Memphis, TN: Mississippi River Flood Control Association, 1927.

The Association's report on one of the most devastating floods in modern history, which damaged nearly 13 million acres of flood plain and nearby areas.

(79) *Official Report of the Proceedings of the Mississippi River Improvement Convention: Held in Saint Louis, Missouri, on October 26th, 27th and 28th, 1881: Including Letters from Distinguished Men throughout the Country.* Saint Louis: Great Western Print. Co., 1881.

The beginning of the building of flood walls in urban areas sometimes equaling those of Troy, as well as heightened construction of levees throughout the region.

(80) L.T. Berthe. *Old Man River Speaks: The Birds Point – New Madrid Floodway, the Most Highly Controversial Engineering Proposal of the Jadwin Plan for Mississippi River Flood Control, Reviewed by the Generals, the Private, and Old Man River.* Charleston, MO: 1937.

Studies on flood control often led to counterblasts and in the long run the Mississippi seemed always to have the final say as this pamphlet's cover would attest.

(81) A. Jaminet. *Physical Effects of Compressed Air, and of the Causes of Pathological Symptoms Produced on Man, by Increased Atmospheric Pressure Employed for the Sinking of Piers, in the Construction of the Illinois and St. Louis Bridge over the Mississippi River at St. Louis, Missouri.* Saint Louis, MO: R. & T.A. Ennis, Stationers and Printers, 1871.

Not much was known about the mysterious caissons disease which overtook the workmen who toiled under tremendous pressures and knew nothing about slow decompression. Jaminet's work was one of the earliest treatises.

(82) Herbert Hoover. *Letter to Donald T. Wright.* Washington, D.C.: 1932.

A telegram from the White House to the editor of the *Waterways Journal*, the nation's historic trade journal for river commerce stressing federal commitment to the river system: *"The development of the natural water channels of the United States has long been a primary interest of mine. These channels, systematically modernized, are of the greatest benefit to agriculture and industry as a means of economical transportation of bulk goods. Twice as much work on these inland waterways has been accomplished in the last three years as in any comparable period in our history." Herbert Hoover, November 18, 1932.*

(83) Charles Ellet, Jr. ***Report and Plan for a Wire Suspension Bridge, Proposed to be Constructed Across the Mississippi River at Saint Louis.*** Philadelphia: William Stavely & Co., Printers, 1840.

The first plan for a bridge linking the two halves of the continent across the Mississippi called for a graceful suspension. Never built, this work shows what could have been a generation before the first bridge was finally constructed.

(84) C.M. Woodward. ***A History of the St. Louis Bridge; Containing a Full Account of Every Step in its Construction and Erection, and Including the Theory of the Ribbed Arch and the Tests of Materials.*** Saint Louis, MO: G.I. Jones and Company, 1881.

A massive study of the Eads Bridge, almost forgotten today but in many St. Louis houses at the time through subscription, with detailed plans, charts and early photographs.

(85) Chauncey I. Filley. ***Invitation to the Formal Opening of Eads Bridge.*** 1874.

On the Fourth of July, 1876, President Grant dedicated the St. Louis Bridge which came to be known as Eads Bridge. Steamboats congregated under the piers and blew grand salutes with their whistles...as the locomotives immediately started moving westward. The beginning and an ending in many ways of a new form of transportation gradually displacing an older one as Americans switched direction and focus from north and south to east and west.

(86) James B. Eads. ***Report on the Mississippi Jetties by James B. Eads, Chief Engineer.*** New York: 1876.

If Eads had done nothing else, his work on the hydraulics and improvement of the currents of the river would be considered monumental in preserving trade and commerce through better navigation.

(87) James B. Eads. ***Physics and Hydraulics of the Mississippi River: Report of U.S. Levee Commission.*** New Orleans, LA: Picayune Steam Job Print, 1876.

This is yet another of Eads' studies on the powerful forces of the Mississippi at its journey's end.

Mike Fink, the Ohio Boatman.

See Item 105

Poetry, Humor, Stories

The muse of the Mississippi has inspired many writers, giving us one clear candidate to the "great American novel" as well as numerous poems, books of humor, historical Americana and regional anecdote. This is a literature of a type all to itself and includes great novelists, essayists and poets who became intoxicated with their subject and never strayed far from it.

(88) Mark Twain. ***Adventures of Tom Sawyer.*** Chicago: American Publishing Company, 1876.

First edition, first issue. (BAL 3369) Twain owed his genius to Hannibal and the Mississippi – his masterpieces stemmed from the setting. He in turn heard or read the regional humor of Robb, or the *Crockett Almanacs,* which heavily inform his art.

(89) Mark Twain. ***Adventures of Huckleberry Finn (Tom Sawyer's Comrade).*** New York: Charles L. Webster and Company, 1885.

First American edition, early issue. (BAL 3415) With the first British edition of 1884 (BAL 3414)

(90) Mark Twain. ***Life on the Mississippi.*** London: Chatto & Windus, 1883.

The British edition preceded the American as the true first printing.

(91) Hezekiah Butterworth. ***Zigzag Journeys on the Mississippi: From Chicago to the Islands of the Discovery.*** Boston: Estes and Lauriat, 1892.

A collection of anecdotal tales and musings forming part of a broader series.

(92) T.S. Eliot. **Four Quartets.** New York: Harcourt, Brace, and Company, 1943.

From the poet's *"The Dry Salvages"*:

I do not know much about gods; but I think the river
Is a strong brown god – sullen, untamed and intractable,
Patient to some degree, at first recognized as a frontier;
Useful, untrustworthy, as a conveyor of commerce;
Then only a problem confronting the builder of bridges.
The Problem once solved, the brown god is forgotten
By the dwellers in cities – ever, however, implacable,
Keeping his seasons and rages, destroyer, reminder
Of what men choose to forget.

A native of St. Louis, Eliot could write such words firsthand from life's experience in the old river town.

(93) Frederick Way, Jr. **The Saga of the Delta Queen.** Cincinnati, OH: Picture Marine Publishing Company, 1951.

Way was one of the great modern river writers who participated in the history of the subject. He was also an important collector of steamboat diaries, lore and especially photographs. All of his books were bestsellers in the river genre.

(94) Frederick Way, Jr. **The Log of the Betsy Ann.** New York: Robert M. McBride & Company, 1933.

(95) Frederick Way, Jr. **Pilotin' Comes Natural.** New York: Farrar & Rinehart, 1943.

Way was the author of *The Allegheny* for the *Rivers of America* series. He also produced many editions of a standard reference book on river vessels, *Way's Packet Directory.*

(96) Walter Havighurst. Upper Mississippi: **A Wilderness Saga.** New York: Farrar & Rinehart, 1937.

This is one of the earliest volumes of the *Rivers of America* series, telling of the Scandinavian-American communities of the Upper Mississippi.

(97) Harper's New Monthly Magazine. Vol. 23 (Dec. 1858 – May 1859). New York: Harper & Brothers, 1859.

A cartoonist's parody of the early river panoramas was presented in the December, 1858 issue by a satirist named Arrowsmith. Mark Twain even later satirized a panorama in *Life on the Mississippi.*

(98) Irvin Anthony. ***Paddle Wheels and Pistols.*** Philadelphia: Macrae, Smith, & Company, 1929.

(99) Virginia Eifert. ***Three Rivers South: The Story of Young Abe Lincoln.*** New York: Dodd, Mead, & Company, 1953.

Eifert came from Springfield, Illinois and published numerous books and won many awards for reaching young people with her historical treatments of the river – especially her "Young Lincoln" trilogy. This work was illustrated by Thomas Hart Benton.

(100) Virginia Eifert. ***Mississippi Calling.*** New York: Dodd, Mead, & Co., 1957.

Eifert's work is infused with biography – of settlers and pioneers, of the many peoples of the Mississippi Valley, but ultimately of the river itself.

(101a) Ben Lucien Burman. ***Children of Noah: Glimpses of Unknown America.*** New York: Messner, 1951.

(101b) Ben Lucien Burman. ***Mississippi.*** New York: John Day Co., 1929.

(101c) Ben Lucien Burman. ***Steamboat Round the Bend.*** Boston: Little, Brown, and Co., 1936.

(101d) Ben Lucien Burman. ***Rooster Crows for Day.*** New York: The World Publishing Co., 1947.

(101e) Ben Lucien Burman. ***Big River to Cross: Mississippi Life Today.*** New York: John Day Co., 1940.

(102) Ben Lucien Burman. ***Blow for a Landing.*** New York: John Day, 1938.

Burman was hailed as the "re-discoverer of the Mississippi in the twentieth century." He was convinced when he began writing that there were still good tales to tell about the colorful people on the rivers and went on a crusade to accomplish a body of writing that was best-selling across America. His wife, Alice Caddy, illustrated many of his works.

(103) Carl Carmer. *Songs of the Rivers of America.* New York: Farrar & Rinehart, Inc., 1942.

One of the editors of the *Rivers of America* series also edited this collection of songs for the series, which went through only one printing and became one of the scarcest titles in the splendid series, a landmark of the mid-twentieth century American appetite for Americana of all kinds. What more creative series could one evoke than that for rivers?

(104) *Davy Crockett's Almanack, of Wild Sports of the West, and Life in the Backwoods. Vol.1, No.2.* Nashville, TN: 1836.

The *Crockett Almanacs* spanned three decades and in their pages preserved much southern folklore and humor, dialect and illustration, ostensibly surrounding the life of Crockett and his friends, such as Mike Fink. (See Item 105)

(105) *Davy Crockett's Almanack, of Wild Sports of the West, Life in the Backwoods, Sketches of Texas, and Rows on the Mississippi. Vol. 1, No. 4.* Nashville, TN: Heirs of Col. Crockett, 1838.
Many of the Crockett exploits focused on the Mississippi – he waded it, he swam it and fought giant catfish in it, he navigated it in fantastic vessels – all creating a backdrop for the frontiersman's exploits.

(106) *Ben Hardin's Crockett Almanac, Rows Sprees and Scrapes in the West; Life and Manners in the Backwoods; and Terrible Adventures on the Ocean.* New York: Turner & Fisher, 1842.

(107) Hodding Carter. *Rivers of America: Lower Mississippi.* New York: Rinehart & Company, Inc., 1942.

The Mississippi needed two volumes for the *Rivers of America* series – two distinct rivers thus were depicted with different cultures and history. This circumstance seemed natural to the editors but was somewhat criticized. The *Upper Mississippi* volume was felt in need of revision and to be more focused; the companion volume by Carter for the lower half of the river was praised as one of the most significant works of its day.

(108) G.W. Ogden. *Tennessee Todd.* New York: A.S. Barnes & Company, 1903.

(109) John Gill. *The Mississippi: November 7, 1837.* Kirkwood, MO: The Printery, 1986.

A description of the river as it passed through Alton, Illinois, the night Elijah Lovejoy was murdered for defending his press, about to be cast in the murky depths.

(110) Richard Bissell. *High Water. Boston: Little, Brown, and Company,* 1954.

Harvard-educated Bissell had a varied career before settling down to writing about his experiences as a towboat pilot on the Upper Mississippi – the first since Mark Twain.

See Item 112

Objects and Artifacts:
The Great River's Material Culture

The Mercantile Library has collected various photographic and manuscript archives from the steamboat and towboat companies which have been seasoned with many artifacts – ship bells, pilot-wheels, duck decoys, and a myriad of other emblems of river life, including these posters, models, original architectural elements and tools of the trade, such as the Lead Line (item 123), all vestiges of a past glory and proud enhancements to a modern library research collection.

(111) *The New and Splendid Passenger Steamer Ruth!* Original Dock Advertisement. 1863.

(112) *Various Promotional Brochures.* Streckfus Steamboat Line and St. Louis & Tennessee River Packet Co.

(113) *"Along the Upper Mississippi via the Popular Jo Line Steamers" Souvenir.* Chicago: Rand, McNally & Co.

(114) *Log Book, Memphis Harbor, July 15, 1878 – October 31, 1883*

(115) *Enrollment Certificate for the Steamboat "Grace Darling", 1856*

(116) *Manifest of the Steamboat "James Howard".* St. Louis, 1875.

Manifests like this one documented the complex business of operating a steamboat in 19th century St. Louis. The load described here – 2,056 bales – is far smaller than the record-breaking 7,701 bales the *James Howard* would carry from St. Louis to New Orleans on another trip in 1875.

(117) *River Test for Sections of the Mississippi,* mid-20th century.

Portions of the river are drawn by a river pilot on a roll of paper to show his or her knowledge and expertise of the channel. Such artifacts hearken back to the early days of licensing river pilots who had to know river depths and charts, snags and banks, backwards and forwards. As one old captain once told this author, "John, what you do is just keep the boat in the middle of the stream."

(118) Glenn S. Hensley. ***Keelboat model.*** St. Louis: 2003.

Keelboats were used along the Mississippi River and its tributaries until the advent of steamboats. Even at speeds of eight miles per hour, a steamboat had obvious advantages over the keelboat that took its crew three months working with poles, oars and tow ropes to bring a cargo from New Orleans to St. Louis.

(119) Glenn S. Hensley. ***Steamer "Erastus Wells" model.*** St. Louis: 2008.

In December of 1907 the city of St. Louis launched a steam-powered harbor boat to carry city personnel and visitors on inspection trips along the riverfront. A *St. Louis Globe-Democrat* article at the time praised the boat's expected speed of 12 miles per hour against the current and declared it to be "one of the finest harbor boats in the western waters, second to none in the country."

(120) ***Steamboat Whistles.*** Ca. 1880.

(121) ***Keno Goose and Chuck-a-Luck Cup.*** Ca.1880.

These common gambling devices were used on the steamboat *Grand Republic* in 1876. (See Item 19)

(122) ***Fisherman's License Buoy.*** Owner: E. King, St. Charles, Missouri. Early 20th century.

(123) ***Lead Line for "Marking Twain".***

This lead weight tied to a rope marked with colored cloth to indicate the depths of the water would be dropped over the side – a process referred to as "Marking Twain". This process, so essential to the safe navigation of the constantly changing mighty Mississippi, was the inspiration for Samuel Clemens' pen name. (See Item 40)

(124) Edward R. Ruch. ***Pilothouse model.*** Ca.1969.

Based on the pilothouse for the *Golden Eagle*. (See Item 44)

(125) ***Steamboat Finial.*** Late nineteenth century.

(126) ***Historical Marker, Site of the American Fur Company and Boatmen's Exchange Building,*** Ca. 1948.

In 1811 the first expedition of John Jacob Astor's American Fur Company left St. Louis from the riverfront. On the same site in 1868 the Boatmen's Exchange Building was erected and embellished with relief sculptures of steamboats.

(127) ***Steamboat Bell Pull,*** Ca. 1890.

This pilothouse bell pull was made for the steamboat *Belle Calhoun*.

(128) ***Important Events of the Century,*** 1876.

A commercial directory and reference that was made available to passengers in a steamboat library marked "Property of this Steam Boat."